To my babies
Sophie,
Clover and Luke

Kingfisher Books, Grisewood & Dempsey Ltd,
Elsley House, 24–30 Great Titchfield Street,
London W1P 7AD

First published in paperback in 1992 by Kingfisher Books
10 9 8 7 6 5 4 3 2
Originally published in hardback in 1991 by Kingfisher Books

BRITISH LIBRARY CATALOGUING-IN-PUBLICATION DATA
A catalogue record for this book is available
from the British Library

ISBN 0 86272 870 3

Phototypeset by Southern Positives and Negatives (SPAN),
Lingfield, Surrey
Printed in Hong Kong

TESSA DAHL

BABIES BABIES BABIES

ILLUSTRATED BY
SIOBHAN DODDS

Kingfisher Books

Do all baby animals grow in their mummies' tummies?

Well, Sam, lots of animals grow their babies
in their tummies. Dogs, cats, horses,
cows and even whales do.

But birds lay eggs in their nests,

and most frogs

and fish lay eggs in water.

Will our baby be born with its clothes on, Mummy?

Oh no, Sophie, our baby will be born with nothing on at all.

But zebra foals
are born with
all their stripes,

puppies are born
with all their fur,

squirrel babies
have no fur at all

and baby hedgehogs are born without spikes
but grow white ones in a few hours.

Will our baby eat toast and jam?

Oh no, Sam, new babies can only drink milk,
either from the mother's breast or from a bottle.

But most baby birds
are fed worms
and insects,

tiny caterpillars
eat leaves,

and lots of baby animals, puppies,
calves, foals, monkeys and even
baby camels, are fed milk by their
mothers – but not from a bottle.

How many babies will we have, Mummy?
I want you to have twins.

I'm only having one baby, Sophie. Most people
only have one, although some mothers have two
or three, which is very hard work.

Sheep sometimes have three lambs, often
two, but most of all, one.

But dogs have any number of puppies
from one to twenty,

grass snakes can lay up to fifty eggs
which hatch into baby snakes,

and fish have hundreds of brothers
and sisters hatching all at once.

Will we help to look after the baby?

Yes, Sophie, we'll all take care of it.

But with sticklebacks, only the father looks after the babies,

tiger cubs are taken care of by
their mothers, not their fathers,

wolves live in packs and all the
wolves look after the wolf cubs,

and baby turtles don't have
anyone to look after them.

Can animals change too?

Some do, Sophie, but not many.

A caterpillar becomes a chrysalis
which turns into a butterfly,

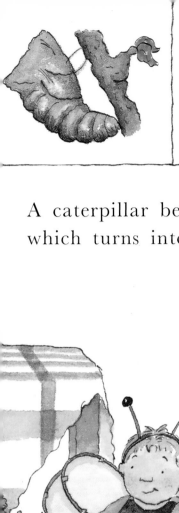

maggots turn into
bluebottles or flies

and tadpoles grow front
and back legs, then their
tails disappear and they
become frogs.

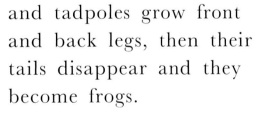

Mummy, when will our baby be able
to walk in the park?

When our baby is about six months,
which is half a year old, it will
learn to crawl, Sam, but it won't
be able to walk until it's one
or more.

Baby birds learn to fly at all
sorts of different ages – from a
thrush fledgling at two weeks all
the way to a cygnet at sixteen
weeks old, just as it is growing
into a swan.

How do animals push their babies, Mummy?

They don't, Sophie, they carry them.

How?

Well, crocodiles carry their babies in their mouths,

kangaroos hop around with their baby joeys in their pouches,

beaver kits hold onto their mothers' fur when they go for a swim,

and baboon babies cling onto their mothers' tummies until they are old enough to ride piggy-back.

How long before our baby is born?

Well, human mothers carry their babies
in their tummies for nine months,
so do cows.

Puppies are born after two months
and a bit,

foals take eleven months to grow in the mother horse's tummy,

and elephant calves stay in their mothers' tummies for twenty-two months,

| 7 | 8 | 9 | 10 | 11 | 12 |

which is nearly two years.

| 19 | 20 | 21 | 22 | 23 | 24 |

When will we have grown enough
to be grown up, Mummy?

A human can leave home at anytime from
sixteen years old, but humans haven't
finished growing up by then, it takes far longer.

But a mouse leaves its mother
at around twenty days,

a puppy doesn't need its
mother from eight weeks,

and polar bear cubs
leave home when they are
about one year old.

Will our baby go to bed at the same time as us, Mummy?

No, I'm afraid it won't. New babies sleep on and
off all day and night. Usually when they wake up, they
cry because they are hungry.

But most baby birds need feeding all
day and stay awake squawking for food,
fox cubs sleep all day and are awake
all night, while fish babies never sleep.

Mummy, will you kiss and cuddle our baby too?

Oh yes, kisses and cuddles are very important. A cat licks its kittens which is like kissing but cleans them too,

a mother pig pushes her piglets with her snout to cuddle them up close,

and gorillas cuddle their babies all the time.

But some animals can't kiss or cuddle
which must be very lonely. Before you
fall asleep tonight, why don't you
think which ones can and which ones can't.

Goodnight, my little animals.